Christian Prayer Ways

A Workbook of 26 Prayer Ways to Deepen Your Relationship With God

Kathy Bernstrom Lerfald, M.A.
Christian Spiritual Director
Life Coach & Author

Copyright © 2018 Kathy Bernstrom Lerfald. See Page 2 for permission guidelines.

Kathy Bernstrom Lerfald is a Christian spiritual director, personal life coach, author, and founder of Sacred Living. One of her specialties is *prayer ways*, sharing with others the breadth and depth of communication with God.

Christian Prayer Ways: A Workbook of 26 Prayer Ways to Deepen Your Relationship With God
Copyright © 2018 by Kathy Lerfald Bernstrom
All rights reserved. Cannot be copied in its entirety but up to 10 individual pages can be copied for individual use, Bible study groups and church purposes (up to 25 copies of each of the 10 pages).
Contact: christianprayer@pobox.com
ISBN: 978-0-9801187-8-0
Publisher: S&C Resources, St. Paul, Minnesota
ChristianPrayerWays.com

Some scriptures taken from THE MESSAGE. Copyright © 1993, 1994, 1995, 1996, 2000, 2001, 2002. Used by permission of NavPress Publishing Group.'

Copyright © 2018 Kathy Bernstrom Lerfald. See Page 2 for permission guidelines.

A Note from Kathy

Welcome to Christian Prayer Ways: A Workbook of 26 Prayer Ways to Deepen Your Relationship With God. Thank you for taking the time and making the investment in your prayer life. This workbook is for your use as you explore the 26 different Christian ways to pray using the alphabet as your guide.

As a spiritual director I ask people to REFLECT on their Christian lives, and as a life coach I ask them to take ACTION.

This workbook offers you both.

Try the prayer way even if (at first) it feels unfamiliar or even uncomfortable. It truly will strengthen and stretch your prayer muscles. And let's face it. You will connect with some of the prayer ways, and some you never will because it just isn't who you are or want to be. But thanks for trying each one. It could be meaningful and surprisingly fun!

After each prayer way, I give you space to reflect on the experience. Important questions to ask yourself in this portion might include:

Overall how was this prayer way experience for me?

Did it bring me closer to God? Or was it so different or uncomfortable that, at least in this time in my life, the prayer way itself got in the way?

What did I learn about myself in this prayer way?

What did I learn about God in this prayer way?

What did I learn about the connection that God and I share?

Copyright © 2018 Kathy Bernstrom Lerfald. See Page 2 for permission guidelines.

At first glance, this workbook may seem simplistic. And, in some ways, it is. Playful too. Prayer is not meant to be an arduous task but something that flows from us in a natural way. I can, however, assure you that if you delve into these prayer ways, you will find them to be quite profound.

These Christian prayer ways have one purpose and that is to facilitate the connection – the relationship – between you and God. To deepen your relationship!

Thanks again, and I'd love to hear from you. Any feedback would be greatly appreciated. I want this workbook to be a helpful encouragement to you in your Christian prayer life.

Warmly,

Kathy

Kathy Bernstrom Lerfald

> *Prayer is simply a two-way conversation between you and God.*
> *Billy Graham (1918-2018)*

Contact: christianprayer@pobox.com

Note: I do use some symbolism and anthropomorphism (assigning human attributes to God) as avenues of connection with God. We do know that God is spirit and not human but sometimes it just helps!

Copyright © 2018 Kathy Bernstrom Lerfald. See Page 2 for permission guidelines.

Table of Contents

A	A-C-T-S Prayer	....	6
B	Breath Prayer	....	8
C	Childhood Prayer	....	10
D	Dialogue Prayer	....	12
E	Everyday Prayer	....	14
F	Finger Labyrinth Prayer	....	16
G	Glance & Gaze Prayers	....	18
H	Historic Prayer	....	20
I	Imagination Prayer	....	24
J	Jesus Prayer	....	26
K	Kneeling Prayer	....	28
L	Letter to God Prayer	....	30
M	Music Prayer	....	32
N	Nature Prayer	....	34
O	One-Word Prayer	....	36
P	Praying in Pictures	....	38
Q	Quiet Prayer	....	40
R	Rosary Prayer	....	44
S	Scripture Prayer	....	46
T	Thin Place Prayer	....	48
U	Unwork Prayer	....	50
V	Valiant Prayer	....	52
W	Water Prayer	....	54
X	X-treme Prayer	....	56
Y	Yelling Prayer	....	58
Z	Zebra Prayer	....	60

Copyright © 2018 Kathy Bernstrom Lerfald. See Page 2 for permission guidelines.

A-C-T-S Prayer

This is a classic model for prayer. ACTS is an acronym representing:

A = Adoration

> To adore God – to worship God – to praise God for being your Creator, your Redeemer, your _____. (fill in)

C = Confession

> To confess your sins – to "clear away the path" of anything that is between you and God.

T = Thanksgiving

> To thank God for _____. (fill in)

S = Supplication

> To ask God regarding your own needs, the needs of others, and the needs of our world.

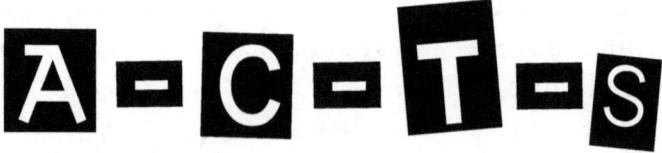

Copyright © 2018 Kathy Bernstrom Lerfald. See Page 2 for permission guidelines.

Write your A-C-T-S prayer here:

_____
_____
_____
_____
_____
_____
_____
_____
_____
_____
_____

Reflections on A-C-T-S Prayer:

_____
_____
_____
_____
_____
_____
_____

Copyright © 2018 Kathy Bernstrom Lerfald. See Page 2 for permission guidelines.

Breath Prayer

This is a prayer that you can say in one breath. It can come from a verse in the Bible, from your heart's desire, from a hymn or song – whatever you wish to pray *in one breath*.

Some examples would be:

- My hope is in you, loving God.
- Grant me your peace, Holy Spirit.
- Jesus, you are my strength.
- I am weary, God.
- Lord Jesus, help me to feel loved.
- The Lord will be my confidence. (Proverbs 3:26)
- I want to know you, Christ, and the power of your resurrection. (Philippians 3:10)
- I love you, Lord.

Write your breath prayer here:

_____
_____
_____
_____
_____
_____
_____
_____

Reflections on Breath Prayer:
_____
_____
_____
_____
_____
_____
_____
_____
_____
_____
_____
_____

Scripture has a lot to say about breath. If you'd like to study this, look up breath in a Bible concordance or online.

Copyright © 2018 Kathy Bernstrom Lerfald. See Page 2 for permission guidelines.

Childhood Prayer

Do you remember the prayers you said as a child? Our dinner prayer was, "Come, Lord Jesus, be our guest and let these gifts to us be blessed." Resurrect the prayers you spoke as a child and pray them now with an adult heart and understanding. "Come, Lord Jesus …"

_____
_____
_____
_____
_____
_____
_____

Pray it today … slowly … slowly.

Reflections on Childhood Prayer:

_____
_____
_____
_____
_____
_____
_____
_____

Copyright © 2018 Kathy Bernstrom Lerfald. See Page 2 for permission guidelines.

There are many wonderful children's prayer books available on Amazon and at bookstores throughout the country, and there is so much to be experienced through their use now as adults.

Here is an example of a traditional children's bedtime prayer:

> **Now I lay me down to sleep,**
> **I pray the Lord my soul to keep:**
> **May God guard me through the night**
> **And wake me with the morning light.**
> **Amen**

And a children's prayer of invitation:

> **Lord, here is my Bible,**
> **Here is this quiet room,**
> **Here is this quiet time**
> **And here am I.**
>
> **Open my eyes; open my mind;**
> **Open my heart; and speak.**

From: The Lion Book of Children's Prayers, Lion Publishing, Compiled by Mary Batchelor © 1983

Copyright © 2018 Kathy Bernstrom Lerfald. See Page 2 for permission guidelines.

D Dialogue Prayer

Write down a dialogue between you and God. Write out your words. Write out what you think God's words might be. Continue to dialogue with God.

God:_____
_____

Me:_____
_____

God:_____
_____

Me:_____
_____

God:_____
_____
_____

Me:_____
_____

Copyright © 2018 Kathy Bernstrom Lerfald. See Page 2 for permission guidelines.

Ask yourself these important questions:

1. Are the words I'm praying right at this moment representing my true thoughts and feelings? Am I being authentic with God?

2. Are God's words representing the loving and just biblical God? You may need some counsel on this.

Reflections on Dialogue Prayer:
_____
_____
_____
_____
_____
_____
_____
_____

E Everyday Prayer

So, you're in the kitchen washing dishes …
So, you're in class at college …
So, you're sitting at your desk at work …
So, you're mowing the lawn …

Ask yourself these questions:

How can what I'm doing right *now* become a prayer?

What might God want to hear from me at this very moment?

What would I want to share with God just as I'm doing this very ordinary life thing?

What is God saying to me?

What did you choose as your everyday prayer?

_____
_____
_____
_____
_____
_____
_____

Copyright © 2018 Kathy Bernstrom Lerfald. See Page 2 for permission guidelines.

Reflections on Everyday Prayer:

_____
_____
_____
_____
_____
_____
_____
_____
_____
_____
_____
_____
_____
_____
_____

Seen as a task or a prayer?

A man I know told me,

*"When I mow the lawn,
I am tending God's garden."*

I see it as a task. He sees it as a prayer.
Big difference, huh?

F Finger Labyrinth Prayer

Labyrinths were walked by Christians in Medieval times and are being rediscovered in the Christian church today.

A labyrinth is not a maze, because in a labyrinth there is only one way in (as you move yourself to the center) and one way out.

It is very difficult to quiet oneself in our world, and a labyrinth is meant to be a rhythmic *quieter* of our hearts and minds. It is used for relaxation, for mediation and for prayer.

Do you have a labyrinth near you? Some churches or cathedrals have them. Some hospitals have them in their outdoor gardens.

If you know of a labyrinth nearby, go walk it and quietly open your heart to God as you follow its path.

A finger labyrinth is located on the next page. Notice the cross shape in the center. Run your finger slowly through the labyrinth.

What prayers do you speak as you quiet yourself before God?

Labrinyth image courtesy of labrinythsociety.org

Reflections on Finger Labyrinth Prayer:

_____
_____
_____
_____
_____
_____
_____
_____
_____
_____

Copyright © 2018 Kathy Bernstrom Lerfald. See Page 2 for permission guidelines.

G Glance & Gaze Prayers

Sometimes a simple glance toward God is a prayer filled with all kinds of unspoken *stuff*. And sometimes the circumstance may call for an extended gaze.

Remember the last time you gazed at a beautiful sunset? Your sleeping baby? Your newly restored classic car?

What was in that gaze?

Awe?
Appreciation?
Amazement?
Mystery?

How much more could that gaze be when it involves your relationship with God?

Read how St. Jane de Chantal (1572-1641) expresses glance:

> *In the midst of many activities that you experience each day, unite your will to God's as often as you can either by a simple, loving glance at God, or by a few words spoken quietly and cast into God's heart.*

Cast your glance at God throughout the day.

I think it may be important to make this a physical glance, so you can choose to look down, look within, look up, look out – wherever **you** tend to envision God.

Spend some time in an extended gaze at God.

Reflections on Glance & Gaze Prayers:
_____
_____
_____
_____
_____
_____
_____
_____
_____

And, if you're just stuck, this verse can be of comfort:

If you don't know how or what to pray, it doesn't matter. He (God's Spirit) does our praying in and for us, making prayer out of our wordless sighs, our aching groans. He knows us far better than we know ourselves ... and keeps us present before God.

Romans 8:26-29
(The Message)

Copyright © 2018 Kathy Bernstrom Lerfald. See Page 2 for permission guidelines.

Historic Prayer

There are some profound prayers that have come down to us through history. Perhaps you come from a tradition of written prayers or perhaps your practice is that of spontaneous prayers.

Here are a few historic, written prayers. Pray them now and see if the writer's words, thoughts and feelings might just be yours as well.

Francis of Assisi 1182-1226
For Peace
Lord, make me an instrument of your peace.
Where there is hatred, let me sow love.
Where there is injury, let me sow pardon.
Where there is doubt, let me sow faith.
Where there is despair, let me give hope.
Where there is darkness, let me give light.
Where there is sadness, let me give joy.
O divine master, grant that I may
not try to be comforted, but to comfort;
not try to be understood, but to understand;
not try to be loved, but to love.
Because it is in giving that we receive,
in forgiving that we are forgiven,
and in dying that we are born to eternal life.

Teresa of Avila 1515-1582
Stubbornness
Although I have often abandoned you, O Lord, you have never abandoned me. Your hand of love is always outstretched towards me, even when I stubbornly look the other way. And your gentle voice constantly calls me, even when I obstinately refuse to listen.

Brother Lawrence 1611-1691
A Constant Prayer
My God, here I am, my heart devoted to you. Fashion me according to your heart.

Soren Kierkegaard, 1813-1855
Christ the Hiding Place
The birds have their nests and the foxes their holes. But you were homeless, Lord Jesus, with nowhere to rest your head. And yet you were a hiding-place where the sinner could flee. Today you are still such a hiding-place, and I flee to you. I hide myself under your wings, and your wings cover the multitude of my sins.

St. Patrick (fourth & fifth centuries)
Christ Be With Me
Christ with me, Christ before me, Christ behind me,
Christ in me, Christ beneath me, Christ above me,
Christ on my right, Christ on my left,
Christ where I lie, Christ where I sit, Christ where I arise,
Christ in the heart of everyone who thinks of me,
Christ in the mouth of every one who speaks to me,
Christ in every eye that sees me,
Christ in every ear that hears me.
Salvation is of the Lord.
Salvation is of the Christ.
May your salvation, Lord, be ever with us.

Copyright © 2018 Kathy Bernstrom Lerfald. See Page 2 for permission guidelines.

The Lord's Prayer
Our Father, who art in heaven,
hallowed be thy name,
thy kingdom come,
thy will be done,
on earth as it is in heaven.
Give us this day our daily bread
and forgive us our debts
as we forgive our debtors,
and lead us not into temptation,
but deliver us from evil,
for thine is the kingdom and the power
and the glory, forever. Amen.
Matthew 6:9-13

Is there another historic prayer that you particularly like? Write it here:

_____
_____
_____
_____
_____
_____
_____
_____
_____
_____
_____
_____

Reflections on Historic Prayer:

_____
_____
_____
_____
_____
_____
_____
_____
_____
_____
_____
_____
_____
_____
_____
_____

<u>Saint Thomas Aquinas (1225-1274)</u>
Grant me, O Lord my God,
a mind to know you,
a heart to seek you,
wisdom to find you,
conduct pleasing to you,
faithful perseverance in waiting for you,
and a hope of finally embracing you.
Amen

Imagination Prayer

Do you think of your imagination as a spiritual practice? Oftentimes we don't, do we?

What if you were to imagine talking with God as …

1. You and God walk on a California beach.
2. You sit like a child in God's lap.
3. You and God enjoy a football game together.
4. You lie comfortably in the palm of God's hand.
5. You and God have a cup of tea together.

A client (who has given her permission to share this with you) once told me that she was so upset and embarrassed about her prayer life.

She wasn't praying the way she was taught to pray (which she assumed was the one true way to pray). I asked her if she shares a connection with God/Jesus/Holy Spirit.

She said sheepishly, "Yes, I do. In my imagination I see Jesus and me sitting on a settee having tea, spending time together and talking."

Wow! What a connection, even though it wasn't the one way she was taught, and she wasn't even sure it "counted."

Be open to your connection with God through your holy imagination!

Copyright © 2018 Kathy Bernstrom Lerfald. See Page 2 for permission guidelines.

In what ways could your imagination enrich your prayer life?
_____
_____
_____
_____
_____
_____
_____

Reflections on Imagination Prayer:
_____
_____
_____
_____
_____
_____
_____

J   Jesus Prayer

There is actually a prayer called The Jesus Prayer, also known as the Prayer of the Heart, and it is perhaps the most time-honored Christian prayer, dating back 1600 years.

There are several versions of this prayer, ranging from the longest 12-word version to a simple 1-word version.

Choose one of these versions and pray it in three phases: first pray it out loud; second pray it silently; and lastly pray it "in your heart."

Lord Jesus Christ, Son of God, have mercy on me a sinner. (classic version)

Lord Jesus Christ, have mercy on me.

Lord Jesus, have mercy on me.

Lord Jesus, have mercy.

Jesus.

Which version(s) of the Jesus Prayer are you most drawn to?

Reflections on Jesus Prayer:

K Kneeling Prayer

Using your body as part of your prayer life may or may not be familiar to you. The simple act of kneeling, intentionally putting our bodies in a different position, can open our minds and hearts to something new.

In the adage, "do one thing different," this could be an easy one thing.

> I have been driven many times to my knees
> by the overwhelming conviction
> that I had nowhere else to go.
> Abraham Lincoln

Other body prayers could include:

Sign of the Cross

The sign of the cross is used by some Christians as a prayer. The open right hand moves to the forehead, then to the stomach/heart area and then across the shoulders from left to right. The movement, thus, becomes the shape of a cross. Often it is accompanied by a prayer recognizing the Trinity:

> In the name of the Father, (forehead)
> and of the Son, (stomach/heart)
> and of the Holy Spirit.
> (across shoulders from left to right)
> Amen

Bert Ghezzi: "The sign of the cross is a very ancient practice and prayer. When you say the words and pray in someone's name you are declaring their presence ..." (catholic.org)

Palms down/Palms up

Practice the palms down/palms up prayer, a prayer of surrendering and receiving. As you place your palms down, you release all your concerns to God. After several moments of surrender, you turn your palms up to receive from God.

Reflections on Kneeling Prayer (and other body prayers):
_____
_____
_____
_____
_____
_____
_____
_____
_____
_____

Copyright © 2018 Kathy Bernstrom Lerfald. See Page 2 for permission guidelines.

Letter to God Prayer

God wants to hear from you! Why not write a letter to God today? I'm going to encourage you to use paper and pen/pencil – not on the computer. Date it, greet God, and then tell God whatever is on your heart and mind. Hold nothing back! Just write and write and write! Get those thoughts and feelings from your head and heart down through your arm, through your fingers and on to paper!

What will you do with this letter once you've written it?
Keep it?
Destroy it?
Read it to your spouse or a friend?
Something else?

My Letter to God:

_____
_____
_____
_____
_____
_____
_____
_____
_____
_____
_____
_____
_____
_____

_____
_____
_____
_____
_____
_____
_____

(continue on additional paper if needed)

Reflections on Letter to God Prayer:
_____
_____
_____
_____
_____
_____
_____
_____
_____
_____
_____

M Music Prayer

Do you enjoy music?

- Instrumental? Vocal?
- Classical? Semi-classical?
- Country? Rock & Roll? Rap?
- Hip-hop? Show tunes?
- Classic hymns?
- Contemporary Christian music?
- Gregorian chants?

Some music touches my soul in such a deep way that I cannot put words to it. I just know that, for me, it is God-inspired. *Danny Boy* and *Ave Maria* are two that immediately come to my mind.

My husband and I have a beautiful rendition of *Ave Maria* that comes from the classic Disney movie Fantasia. It's about five minutes long. And on days when we are really stressed out, we listen to this beautiful classic Christian piece to relax – to be at peace in this world – to release our cares to God – to pray.

During really stressful times, we have been known to listen to it many times!

What music/songs would you include on your *music prayer list*?
_____
_____
_____
_____
_____
_____
_____
_____

Reflections on Music Prayer:
_____
_____
_____
_____
_____
_____
_____
_____

N Nature Prayer

My husband is most connected with God when he is in nature. I don't understand it completely because I'm not wired that way, but he could sit on a tree stump for hours and marvel at God's handiwork.

Nature becomes the bedrock of his prayer. It surrounds him. It speaks to him in its own unique ways (birds singing, loons calling, squirrels chattering, lake water lapping on the shore, the wind whistling through a cottonwood tree, etc.) and draws him close to God, the great Creator.

What part(s) of nature do you most enjoy?

_____
_____
_____
_____
_____

> God writes the Gospel not in the Bible alone,
> but also on trees, and in the flowers and clouds and stars.
> Martin Luther

Try this:

Spend an hour in a setting of natural beauty.

Sit in awe of what God has done in creation.

Copyright © 2018 Kathy Bernstrom Lerfald. See Page 2 for permission guidelines.

Reflections on Nature Prayer:
_____
_____
_____
_____
_____
_____
_____
_____
_____
_____
_____
_____
_____
_____

O One-Word Prayer

If you had to put your prayer into ONE word, what would it be?

Gratitude	Worry	Anger
Despair	Hope	Clarity
Longing	Contentment	Desire
Joy	Curious	Open
John	Lauren	Olivia

Other?

Write that ONE word on a piece of paper, put your hand on top of the paper, and offer that word to God – in silence – in words – in song.

OR take that piece of paper and put it in a jar – a *God Jar* – for safekeeping. It would be like symbolically placing it/him/her into the hands of God.

My one word prayer today is: _____

Reflections on One-Word Prayer:
_____
_____
_____
_____
_____
_____
_____
_____
_____
_____
_____
_____
_____

Copyright © 2018 Kathy Bernstrom Lerfald. See Page 2 for permission guidelines.

P Praying in Pictures

Do you have difficulty putting words to your prayers?

Try praying in pictures!

A colleague of mine was hesitant to even admit that she prayed in pictures. She feared it was a *cut below* praying in words.
What a sense of freedom when she read Morton Kelsey's book on prayer. He writes about praying in pictures.

Don't worry about putting thoughts into words. See the person, the situation, whether in celebration or pain, and offer that picture to God. No words necessary. The *pictures* are the prayers.

What picture would you like to offer to God today (you could write or draw or paste something here)?

Reflections on Praying in Pictures Prayer:

_____
_____
_____
_____
_____
_____
_____
_____
_____
_____

Q Quiet Prayer

Have you ever seen an old married couple who just sit in the presence of each other? Perhaps they are in a restaurant for dinner, and neither talks to the other.

Maybe they are upset with each other (that's a possibility) or maybe they just like being in the presence of each other – without words – just being.

It's so hard for us to make the switch from *doing* to *being*. Even in our prayer lives we think we have to *do* prayer!

Try this.

Sit with God for 15 minutes or for a while. Close your eyes. Open your eyes. It doesn't matter. Just sit with God in silence. Let go of the pressure to have to come up with words.

Suspend the need for words.

Suspend the need for talk.

**Quiet is not the absence of everything.
It is simply the absence of noise.**

Kathy Bernstrom Lerfald

Reflections on Quiet Prayer:

_____
_____
_____
_____
_____
_____
_____
_____
_____
_____
_____
_____
_____
_____

"Just over a hundred years ago, the French author Charles Peguy, to the annoyance of many readers, published a long poem about Joan of Arc with a number of pages that were entirely blank.

The reason, he explained, was to give the reader 'time to think.' We need blank pages in our lives.

When we make time to pray, we are creating a pocket of stillness amid the rush and hubbub, a precious place in which we can be truly ourselves …"

From: Learn to Pray: A Practical Guide to Faith and Inspiration by Marcus Braybrooke (many faiths represented in this book)

Copyright © 2018 Kathy Bernstrom Lerfald. See Page 2 for permission guidelines.

R Rosary Prayer

Roman Catholic Christians are generally well aware of the rosary. The word itself comes from the Latin word rosarium which means rose garden or garland of roses. The word rosary refers to the actual set of prayer beads and to the prayer itself.

Do you have a rosary?

How do you use it?

Sometimes I just long to hold something while I pray.

But if you are Protestant, like I am, you may have never used a rosary or seldom, if ever, held something while you prayed.

Try this:

Borrow or buy a rosary and learn more specifically about its use, either in full or in part. Perhaps one of your Catholic friends can teach you.

OR do as one of my Protestant friends did and make an adaptation of a rosary for yourself using string and beads. Each of her beads represents a different person in her family, and she prays for each one as she holds the bead.

Rosaries engage our senses,
especially our sense of sight – they are beautiful –
and our sense of touch.

Reflections on Rosary Prayer:
_____
_____
_____
_____
_____
_____
_____
_____
_____
_____
_____
_____
_____
_____
_____

Scripture Prayer

Lectio Divina, pronounced lekt-see-o di-vee-na, is a Latin word for *spiritual* reading. It is a form of prayer that uses scripture in a specific way.

Pick out a few verses of scripture or possibly just one verse. This prayer form is more about going deeper into scripture than the quantity of verses read.

If you need a suggestion, try a verse or verses from Psalm 62:

> Find rest, O my soul, in God alone;
> my hope comes from him.
> He alone is my rock and my salvation;
> he is my fortress, I will not be shaken.
>
> Trust in him at all times, O people;
> pour out your hearts to him,
> for God is our refuge.
>
> One thing God has spoken,
> two things have I heard:
> that you, O God, are strong,
> and that you, O Lord, are loving.

There are four phases to this prayer:

1. Read the scripture aloud several times, slower each time.
2. Spend some time thinking and meditating on the passage, a phrase or one of its words to which you are drawn.
3. Now spend some time letting it *sink into your heart*.
4. Sit in God's presence around what you have read and experienced.

Reflections on Scripture Prayer:
_____
_____
_____
_____
_____
_____
_____
_____

Thin Place Prayer

Some Christians believe there are actual places where it seems God is somehow closer or you experience God's presence in a deeper, more significant way. These are called *thin places*.

I have a few thin places that I've come to recognize over the years: driving alone in the car, taking a shower (see the letter W for Water Prayer), and the first thing in the morning as I'm just waking up.

Margaret Guenther in her book Holy Listening writes about the *thin veil of the morning*, that time when you are not fully asleep and not fully awake, and she writes that this is a time when God can be present in meaningful and significant ways.

What thin place or places do you recognize in your prayer life?
_____
_____
_____
_____
_____
_____
_____
_____

Copyright © 2018 Kathy Bernstrom Lerfald. See Page 2 for permission guidelines.

Reflections on Thin Place Prayer:
_____
_____
_____
_____
_____
_____
_____
_____
_____
_____
_____
_____
_____

U Unwork Prayer

Sometimes we see prayer as work, and sometimes it is! What is the opposite of work? Fun! Play!

If we only understand prayer as work, as duty or obligation, the love connection with God may be lost in translation. Playfulness is missing.

There is only one letter's difference between PRAY and PLAY!

Why not spend an afternoon with God in an unwork/fun/playful way?

What would that mean to you?
_____
_____
_____

Where would you go? What would you do?
_____
_____
_____

What would be a playful way to connect with God?
_____
_____
_____

A woman once told me that she dances the hula as a prayer. It's not work for her. It's sheer joy! A prayerful, playful expression of prayer – an expression of love.

When I was a teenager, I watched a movie on TV on the life of Christ (and haven't seen it since), and in that movie Jesus was playing a form of touch football with his disciples.

Honestly, watching that truly broadened my image of who Jesus was and is. I could add the word *playful* to my description of Jesus, and that made him more human and approachable to me.

If you know the movie I'm referring to, please contact me. I'd love to see it again and will include its title in the next edition of this workbook.

Reflections on Unwork Prayer:
_____
_____
_____
_____
_____
_____
_____
_____
_____
_____
_____
_____
_____

V Valiant Prayer

Valiant is not a word we use much, is it? It means brave – courageous.

Is there a prayer that you would like to pray and you need to be brave and courageous to pray it?

_____
_____
_____
_____
_____

Perhaps it is a BIG ASK of God. Asking God for:

Perhaps it is a BIG LISTEN to hear what God wants to say to you, to ask you to be or do – for yourself – for our world.

Perhaps it is a subject so much deeper than you have ever gone before with God that it is scary to be courageous and bring it up to God.

There's an old reading from an early 1900s philosopher that speaks about a wish that may be deep within you, your heart's desire, which God is calling out from you. It may be so beyond whom you think you are or could be, but God is telling you to *come forth*.

It takes a lot of courage to listen to that *come forth* and then to be or do what God is asking of you.

Is God asking you to *come forth*?

Reflections on Valiant Prayer:

W Water Prayer

Several of my spiritual direction clients have shared with me that they feel a closeness to God in the shower! That somehow they are more *alive* to God when surrounded by water. (Remember T, the Thin Place Prayer?)

I've heard artists say that some of their best inspiration comes while they are in the shower.

There's something about water. Water is a basic element of life, and it is the basic element in our lives as well. We need water to survive.

In our Christian faith, we are baptized with water.

And could the use of water be a *helping element* in our prayers?

Try this:

Next time you are swimming or in the shower or taking a long tub soak, become aware of your connection with God. Is it different than at other times?

Might your *God antennae* be more sensitive when you're in or near water?

*When you wash your hands,
remember your baptism.
Martin Luther*

Reflections on Water Prayer:
_____
_____
_____
_____
_____
_____
_____
_____
_____
_____

Copyright © 2018 Kathy Bernstrom Lerfald. See Page 2 for permission guidelines.

X X-treme Prayer (marathon)

Okay, this may *not* be for the novice pray-er or faint of heart! How about an x-treme prayer?

    Praying for an hour?

    Praying for hours?

Ask yourself:

How might I be changed if I spend 5 hours in a row (for example) praying?

_____
_____
_____
_____
_____

What might God's response be if I *showed up* for a l-o-n-g prayer time?

_____
_____
_____
_____

Copyright © 2018 Kathy Bernstrom Lerfald. See Page 2 for permission guidelines.

Reflections on X-treme Prayer:
_____
_____
_____
_____
_____
_____
_____
_____
_____
_____

Prayer is when you talk to God;
meditation is when you listen to God.
Author Unknown

God speaks in the silence of the heart.
Listening is the beginning of prayer.
Mother Teresa

Pray, and let God worry.
Martin Luther

Let God or be God.
Unknown

Y Yelling Prayer

There are cultures where people go to a mountain top and scream their prayers! While that may not be your style or your interest, perhaps there is something to *screaming out* a prayer.

Could be cathartic and very real before God!

In our more *civilized* society, why not yell a prayer – perhaps scream it into your pillow or scream out in a remote place?

What do you find yourself yelling?

_____
_____
_____
_____
_____
_____
_____
_____

Reflections on Yelling Prayer:
_____
_____
_____
_____
_____
_____
_____
_____
_____
_____

Z Zebra Prayer

It's hard to come up with a prayer way that starts with the letter Z, but I think I've discovered one!

A zebra holds two colors on his/her body – black & white – opposites.

Sometimes we say things like this: "Well, this issue isn't a black and white one," meaning nuanced and not polar opposites.

Try this:

Pray a zebra prayer by holding two seemingly opposite things in your mind and heart as your prayer.

For example, perhaps you hold the opposite feelings of love and indifference for someone – perhaps even for God.

Talk to God about these seemingly contradictory *zebra* thoughts and feelings.

Copyright © 2018 Kathy Bernstrom Lerfald. See Page 2 for permission guidelines.

Reflections on Zebra Prayer:

_____
_____
_____
_____
_____
_____
_____
_____
_____
_____

Closing Thoughts

Well, we've now gone through 26 different prayer ways, using the alphabet as our guide. The purpose of this workbook is to present a variety of different prayer ways or prayer forms.

Did you find yourself being drawn to one, or a few, in particular? Which one or ones?

_____
_____
_____
_____
_____
_____
_____

Thanks so much for your interest in prayer ways. I hope this workbook has been of help to you and that it has and will continue to enrich your prayer life.

Warmly,

Kathy

Kathy Bernstrom Lerfald

Contact: christianprayer@pobox.com

Copyright © 2018 Kathy Bernstrom Lerfald. See Page 2 for permission guidelines.

www.ingramcontent.com/pod-product-compliance
Lightning Source LLC
Chambersburg PA
CBHW060721030426
42337CB00017B/2957